Armchair Puzzlers™

✦ Secret Identities ✦

Sink Back and Solve Away!™

Bob Moog

UNIVERSITY GAMES

Editorial Director: Erin Conley
Copy Director: Maria Llull
Designer: Jeanette Miller

Special thanks to Suzanne Cracraft, Lynn Gustafson, Lisa Yordy,
Emily Jocson and Joe Kwong for their invaluable assistance!

Printed in China.

ISBN 1-57528-958-X

TABLE OF CONTENTS

3

INTRODUCTION

Since childhood, I have been fascinated with the people who create our nation's history. After learning to read with the old Dick and Jane primers, I quickly took a fancy to biographies and to the accomplishments of the world's history makers. I must have appeared rather odd reading the life stories of Andrew Jackson, Alexander Graham Bell and Charlemagne in elementary school, but I just couldn't get enough.

Each person's life story revealed so many experiences that were forgotten over time. Isaac Newton, for example, was an accomplished economist decades after discovering gravity. Alexander Graham Bell, on the other hand, was a renowned composer and researcher of deafness decades before the invention of the telephone. They both had secret identities outside of their professional lives.

This book is about identifying historical figures and contemporary celebrities based on their lesser-known accomplishments. The book is in three sections. Each section uses a different method of description, which gives some insight into the person behind the celebrity.

There are 83 different people from different countries and different eras in this book. Have fun identifying the "secret identities" and then have even more fun stumping your friends and family.

Best regards,

Bob Moog

INSTRUCTIONS

Each page in this book has its own "Secret Identities" puzzle. There are three types of puzzles: Get a Clue, Mysterious Musings and Been There, Done That.

Get a Clue

Use the six clues to figure out the Secret Identity. Try to identify in as few clues as possible.

Mysterious Musings

Giving statements "spoken" from the grave, these Secret Identities are all deceased. The illustrations offer a giant hint to their identities.

Been There, Done That

Like a connect-the-dots game, the clues in this section are made up of associations that will lead you to the correct Secret Identity. Each clue deals with a part of the mysterious person's past.

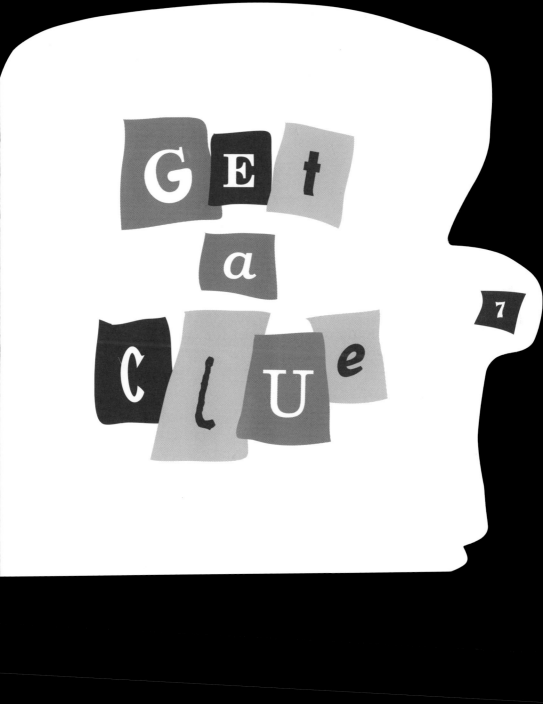

Get a Clue

1. I got my start as a futuristic king of the road.

2. I was born in the 1950s.

3. In 2002, I knew what women wanted.

4. I am not related to Cardinals' pitcher Bob Gibson.

5. Danny Glover thought that I was a lethal weapon in the 1990s.

6. In 2004, my film about the death of a biblical figure was one of the top-grossing films of the year.

8

Get a Clue

1. I attended University of Mississippi law school.

2. My career in law led to a stint in my state's legislature.

3. My stories uncover the legal system and the social system in the South.

4. I write about lawyers, guns and money.

5. *Publisher's Weekly* named me the best-selling author of the 1990s.

6. When my books get made into movies, Tom Cruise, Gene Hackman, Julia Roberts and Matt Damon get meaty starring roles.

Get a Clue

1. I am an American athlete.

2. For more than 20 years, I had a ball at work.

3. I am in the Baseball Hall of Fame.

4. My favorite bird is the oriole.

5. For years, I went to work with my dad and my brother Billy.

6. I surpassed Lou Gehrig's record for consecutive games played.

10

Get a Clue

1. I studied at the University of Maryland.

2. I started my career as a puppeteer.

3. In 1969 I hit the big time on public television with a street full of life-sized puppets.

4. In later life I developed breakthrough television shows like *Fraggle Rock* and *The Storyteller*.

5. If you know my name it is probably because of the street that I built.

6. In the 1970s, my piggish female friend was an international celebrity.

GEt a CLUe

1. I am a living American female.

2. My middle name is Fiona.

3. My brother is also an accomplished actor.

4. I've made nearly as many headlines for my romances with Keifer, Jason and Lyle as I have with my on screen romances with Richard, Dennis, and Hugh.

5. My favorite legal expert is Erin Brockovich.

6. I am a Georgia native and an Academy Award®-winning actress.

Get a Clue

1. I am a living American movie director.

2. My controversial film about Christ isn't called *The Passion of the Christ*.

3. Being raised in New York's Little Italy has influenced my movies.

4. In March 2003, I received the Directors Guild of America's Lifetime Achievement Award.

5. Cameron Diaz, Sharon Stone, Paul Newman and Nicolas Cage have all worked for me.

6. My *Taxi Driver* ran into Cybill Shepherd and Jodie Foster.

Get a Clue

1. I made art my day job.

2. I died in 1987.

3. I have my own museum in Pittsburgh, Pennsylvania.

4. I have no children, but I am called pop.

5. I did a film satire on Frankenstein.

6. Fifteen minutes became a lifetime for me.

1. I was born in Michigan in 1950 and named Steveland Morris.

2. I lost my eyesight when I was an infant, but I didn't lose my musical abilities.

3. My first big hit was "Fingertips" in 1962.

4. During the 1980s, Paul McCartney and I aired together on MTV, living in perfect harmony.

5. I was inducted into the Rock and Roll Hall of Fame in 1989.

6. I once wrote and sang a tribute to Duke Ellington.

Get a Clue

1. I was born in Atlanta, Georgia.

2. My name sounds like royalty.

3. I married Coretta Scott.

4. I wrote *Why Can't We Wait* in 1964.

5. I preached at Ebenezer Baptist Church.

6. I was named after a key Reformation figure.

16

Get a Clue

1. I share my first name with a planet and a Roman goddess.

2. My sister is a professional tennis player.

3. My balls are usually yellow.

4. I share my last name with a singer named Andy.

5. I was born in 1980.

6. I won at Wimbledon in 2000.

17

1. My "Revolution" was not set in Russia.

2. I am nude on an album cover.

3. My mates started as metallic bugs.

4. My son Sean and I were born on the same day of the same month.

5. My first band was The Quarrymen.

6. I'm half of one of the most famous song writing teams of all time.

18

GΕt a ClUe

1. I am a living American male.

2. I grew up in Oakland, California.

3. I'm not a weight lifter, but I won an award for being big.

4. People started talking about me when I fell in love with a mermaid.

5. In my early career, having *Bosom Buddies* was essential.

6. My wife is actress Rita Wilson.

19

GeT a Clue

1. I was born in 1963 in Brooklyn, New York.

2. I attended the University of North Carolina.

3. I worked part-time for a shoe company for nearly 20 years.

4. Although I'm not a pilot, my nickname is "Air."

5. No bull, I am best known as a professional athlete.

6. For three years, people called me a Wizard.

Get a Clue

1. I was born in Fairfield, CT in 1961.

2. My friends knew me as Margaret Mary Emily Ann Hyra when I was a kid.

3. Walter Matthau played my uncle, Albert Einstein, in a movie.

4. In real life, Dennis Quaid and I lived in San Francisco's Pacific Heights in a house that Kent McCarthy bought.

5. I proved to Harry that women can easily fake orgasms.

6. In the movies I've played Lt. Goose's wife, Jim Morrison's girlfriend and the long distance love interest of Jonah's dad.

Get a Clue

1. I was born in Brooklyn, New York in 1935.

2. I am a neurotic, clarinet playing, writer/director/actor.

3. My parents are Mr. and Mrs. Konigsberg.

4. My first screenplay was *What's New, Pussycat?*

5. Diane Keaton worked for me a lot during the 1970s.

6. I've spent the last thirty years exploring my mind's idea of how people relate through a series of films that sometimes work and sometimes don't but I don't care, because the important thing to me is to get these stories and characters out of my head. Oh God, here I go again... It's crazy. Help me.

Get a Clue

1. I was born in Minnesota in 1921 and was called Frances as a child.

2. I got my start at the Chicago World's Fair in 1933 as one of the Gumm Sisters.

3. I was friends with the Rat Pack.

4. I had five husbands, but was never married to Mickey Rooney.

5. My daughters are Liza and Lorna.

6. I sang "(Dear Mr. Gable) You Made Me Love You" to Clark on his 36th birthday.

1. I grew up in the 1930s in orphanages and foster homes.

2. Though I was married to a great athlete and a famous playwright, I'm best known as a movie actress.

3. Billy Joel mentions me in his song, "We Didn't Start The Fire."

4. I'm no doctor, but I tried to cure an itch.

5. I don't know if you know my name, but JFK sure did after I sang to him on his birthday.

6. I was in the first issue of *Playboy*.

24

GEt a CLUe

1. I was born in Santa Monica, California in 1928.

2. I am an American female.

3. A popular drink was named after me.

4. I helped introduce Mr. Bojangles decades before Jerry Jeff Walker's song.

5. During the 1970s I served as Ambassador to Ghana.

6. My married last name is a color.

7. My acting career peaked before I reached puberty.

1. I am best known for my work in the movies.

2. If you've seen *Deliverance*, you've seen my Pop on the river.

3. I helped bring Lara Croft from cyberspace to the silver screen.

4. I won an Academy Award® for playing a sociopathic inmate in a psychiatric hospital.

5. You shouldn't be surprised to find me in a tattoo parlor.

6. My Billy and my Bob were the same person.

26

Get a Clue

1. I spent a good deal of my adult life in a wheelchair.

2. I married my second cousin.

3. The US Constitution was changed after my death.

4. I'm not Monty Hall, but I love to offer New Deals.

5. If Hoover is known for the Great Depression, I'm known for World War II.

6. I was the governor of New York before becoming President of the US.

27

Get a Clue

1. I am best known as an author.

2. I created Gerald McBoing-Boing.

3. I like to rhyme, but I'm no Longfellow.

4. My film *Hitler Lives* won an Oscar® for best documentary.

5. In 1937, I went to Mulberry Street and saw some cool stuff.

6. I invented the term "nerd."

Get a Clue

1. I am best known as a rock musician.

2. I'm no Romeo but I surround myself with heartbreakers.

3. I lent my voice to an episode of *The Simpsons*.

4. My name suggests that I might make a big deal out of nothing.

5. I know an "American Girl" when I see one.

6. In the 1980s, I was a Traveling Wilbury.

29

Get a Clue

1. I am a soulful singer.

2. I appeared on Motown's Tamla label in the 1960s.

3. In 1987, I was the first woman to be inducted into the Rock and Roll Hall of Fame.

4. I appeared in *The Blues Brothers* with Dan Aykroyd and John Belushi.

5. I sang at the inauguration of President Bill Clinton and at the wedding of Vice President Al Gore's daughter, Karenna.

6. Respect is really important to me.

Get a Clue

1. I was born in the late 1970s, and that decade has done wonders for my career.

2. I've modeled for Versace and Calvin Klein.

3. I am known for losing my car, dude.

4. My friends are glad that I've decided to stop punking them.

5. Though I don't use it, my first name is Christopher.

6. Demi Moore knows that my favorite months are May and December.

Get a Clue

1. I was the 1990s queen of entertaining.

2. I share my first name with George Washington's wife.

3. I'm more likely to shop at Kmart® than Target®.

4. In 2004, I was convicted of committing a felony.

32

5. For years, I was a real role model for women.

6. People call me the "Domestic Diva."

1. I am a living American male actor.

2. I was born in Santa Monica in 1971.

3. I know Bilbo Baggins better than you do.

4. "Goonies never say die!" was my first big line.

5. I was called Rudy when I played football for Notre Dame.

6. My mother won an Oscar® for playing Helen Keller.

Get a Clue

1. I was born in Hawaii and raised in Australia.

2. I'm a living redheaded actress.

3. My ex-husband and I have appeared on screen together.

4. Who's afraid of Virginia Woolf? Not me!

5. In *Moulin Rouge!*, I played a cabaret performer.

6. My on-screen love interests have included Ewan McGregor, Jude Law and Matt Dillon.

34

Get a Clue

1. I was born in 1965 and I grew up in Manhattan.

2. My mom and dad were a popular comedy duo in the 1960s.

3. I had a very short gig writing for *Saturday Night Live*.

4. I knew that there was something about Mary.

5. If you know the holiday "Festivus," you know my Pop.

6. There wouldn't be a Zoolander without me.

GET a CLUE

1. I was born in Oklahoma in 1963.

2. I majored in journalism at the University of Missouri.

3. I once worked as the El Pollo Loco chicken, but I'm best known as an actor.

4. In 1991, I found myself in a hotel room with Geena Davis.

5. My wife is more than just one of my "Friends".

6. I sucked blood with Tom Cruise in a 1994 flick.

7. In 2001, I co-starred in the remake of *Ocean's Eleven*.

Mysterious musings

37

Mysterious Musings

"Hi. I was born in Florida, Missouri in 1835. My mother called me Sam and was surprised when I became a steamship captain on the Mississippi River. I had a series of interesting jobs, including a stint in the Confederate Army during the Civil War, before I found my calling as a humorist. During my 50-year career I wrote about many topics, including frogs in California, King Arthur and a couple of boys growing up in Missouri." Do you know my pen name?

Mysterious musings

"I was born the son of a glove maker and a farm girl in Stratford-upon-Avon during the 16th century. I was an actor during my early years and discovered my love for watching, directing and writing plays. My life's work has lasted the test of time and I am considered the most read author on the planet, as well as one of the most quoted." Dost thou knowest my name?

Mysterious musings

"I am known as a man of peace and as a force of change. I did a great deal of my work in a poor Asian country that was under British rule. I don't eat meat and didn't actually eat much at all while making a name for myself. My life's goal was achieved in 1947."

Who am I?

Mysterious m u s i n g s

"I am a well known and often quoted scholar, athlete, musician and politician. My favorite game is Mah-Jongg, and for centuries my words have served as a guide for living. You don't need to know my whole name, my surname will do."

I say, if you guess my name, you will be wiser for the effort.

"When I was born in England in 1820, it wasn't much of an event. But during the Crimean War I made a name for myself. Now I encourage women to contribute to helping the needy. I was a pioneer for social change and I founded a school for midwives and nurses."

Whatzmyname?

42

Mysterious musings

"Buon giorno! I was born in Italy in the 15th century, but accomplished more on the other side of the Atlantic Ocean. My claim to fame came when the Queen of Spain paid me to take three ladies on a long sailing trip to a faraway land."

Whatzmyname?

43

Mysterious musings

"I love to be in the air, just like John Glenn loved it 30 years after me. I am most famous for my trip to Paris,

but fame has not always been my friend. The kidnapping of my son in 1932 was a tragic event that put me back in the world news. I lived in Connecticut and England and I died in Hawaii."

Whatzmyname?

Mysterious m*u*s*i*n*g*s

"I am a Brit who left home at 14 and joined the circus. I learned how to do comedy and became a professional stilt walker. In the 1930s, I made a name for myself in the movies and once played C.K. Dexter Haven to Katharine Hepburn's Tracy Lord. In the 1940s and 1950s I starred in several Alfred Hitchcock films. Although I am known as a man of grace and charm, I ended up dying in 1986 in the farming community of Davenport, Iowa."

My real initials are A.L. but what name do you know me by?

"I had a short, volatile life before my death in 1945, but my single literary effort regarding life during World War II has left a lasting impression on the western world. Movies have been made about the time I spent in Holland. My darkest secrets, including my crush on Peter van Daan, have been exposed."

Whatzmyname?

Mysterious musings

"I never thought my short trip with William Dawes back in the 18th century would impress people enough to have a Massachusetts city named after me, but it did. I went from being a master engraver to the subject of songs and even a Longfellow poem. Ironically, all of the credit should go to my horse, Brown Beauty, who made the dark midnight ride possible."

Giddyup and guess my name.

Mysterious musings

"I would have been famous in history even without Shakespeare's plays and Cecil B. DeMilles' epic 1934 film about me. Known only by my first name, I was a queen in Roman times. I love men and even married my brothers. Although I traveled the Nile River, many have said that I lived my life as if it was a river of denial."

I command you to announce my name.

Mysterious musings

"I was born a subject of the British Empire, but after reading John Locke and Jean-Jacques Rousseau, I decided that man had certain inalienable rights that could not be taken away or denied. I owned a big farm in Virginia and was more interested in architecture and investments than politics. I really admired the French and spent several years in Paris as the American minister to France. I died on the 4th of July, on the same day as my old adversary, John Adams."

Whatzmyname?

Mysterious musings

"My life consisted
of Egyptian love affairs,
chariot races, massive toga
parties, successful military
campaigns and a series of political
wars with my legislature. I
declared myself emperor
for life, and that forced
my enemies to kill me.
My story was told
by Shakespeare and
again by Hollywood."

Whatzmyname?

Mysterious musings

"It is rumored that I was king of the Britons around the 6th century. I lived in Camelot, where I met with my knights and planned to conquer the Saxons and spread Christianity. Tales of me have been told for 1500 years, including a famous story by Sir Thomas Malory. During the 1960s, Walt Disney brought the story of my sword, Excalibur, to children."

Whatzmyname?

Mysterious musings

"I was born Elisabeth Griscom in 1752. I opened
an upholstery shop with my husband in
Philadelphia on Arch Street and quickly became
an expert seamstress. I was married three times,
but my biggest
accomplishment was
the design and creation
of my nation's most
important symbol."

Whatzmyname?

THE STATE OF TEXAS.

"I was a frontier Renaissance man. I could hunt, cook, write, paint, sew and fight. I might have been one of the original Tennessee Volunteers. I fought with General Jackson in the Creek War, served in the US House of Representatives, loved bear hunting and died fighting for Texas independence at the Alamo in 1836."

Whatzmyname?

Mysterious musings

"I got my start in the "Show Me State" in 1852 and met my finish near Deadwood, South Dakota in 1903. I spent my good years digging for gold, drinking in bars and dressing like a man to make it in the rough and tumble West. I was a good shot with a gun and an expert rider, and I was a heroine during the smallpox epidemic of 1878."

Whatzmyname?

Mysterious Musings

"It is fitting that I appear in Mysterious Musings because I disappeared mysteriously in 1937. I am an American role model for women because of my love of adventure and independence as well as my ground-breaking work in a man's field. I attended Columbia University and loved to travel before my disappearance with Frederick Noonan off the coast of New Guinea."

Whatzmyname?

"My work in England in the 17th and 18th centuries was in the field of physics. I taught mathematics at Trinity College in Cambridge for 27 years. *Principia*, published in 1687, described the cosmos and established me as the leading scientist of my time. In later years I became Master of the Mint in London and revised the English monetary system. If I were a fruit, I would be an apple."

Can you guess my name?

Mysterious musings

"I am an 18th century German, best known for my work with music. I love the piano and I am proud to have had Wolfgang Mozart as one of my childhood instructors. You may know me for my wild hair and as the idol of *Peanut's* Shroeder."

Whatzmyname?

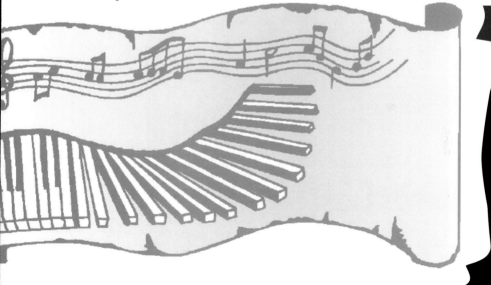

"I have an amazing lineage with a mortal mother and the god Zeus as my father. You probably have heard that I am considered the most beautiful woman on Earth and that a decade-long war was fought in ancient Greece to get me back home. Once returned to my people, I married Menelaus, despite my love for another man."

Whatzmyname?

Mysterious Musings

"I was born in 1412 in a small French village. Although I was not a great political or business leader, I did have a "strong vision" about the direction my people should take. I worked with Charles VII to help him defeat the English and begin his reign as king. My story might have ended there if not for my capture and conviction of heresy by the church. Despite my later canonization, in 1431 I was burned at the stake in Rouen as a relapsed heretic."

Whatzmyname?

Mysterious musings

"Even though I was born in the 15th century, I never realized that I was an original Renaissance Man. I am an Italian inventor, engineer, scientist, painter, sculptor and writer. I loved to draw the human body, study flight, explore physics and paint portraits."

I've got some fresh gnocchi for you if you can guess my name.

Mysterious musings

"I got my start in vaudeville while still a teenager, working for the legendary Florenz Ziegfeld. In 1926 I started writing and starring in off-Broadway plays about sex and sin. The censors hated me and drove me to Hollywood, where I became America's favorite sultry seductress. I played Flower Belle Lee in *My Little Chickadee* and co-starred with Cary Grant in *She Done Him Wrong*. I ended my film career in 1977 with Timothy Dalton as my husband in *Sextette*."

Whatzmyname?

"I had an interesting childhood as an orphan with Aristotle as my tutor. While still a teenager, I was crowned king of my country.

I was ambitious and determined to conquer King Darius and the Persians.

I spent more than a decade building my superior army and cementing my reputation as a strategic military mastermind. I died at the age of 32."

Whatzmyname?

BEEN THERE > < DONE THAT

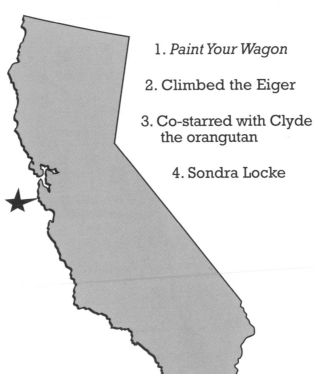

1. *Paint Your Wagon*

2. Climbed the Eiger

3. Co-starred with Clyde the orangutan

4. Sondra Locke

64

BEEN THERE DONE THAT

1. *Guys and Dolls*

2. Paul Whiteman

3. "Chairman of the Board"

4. Hoboken, NJ

BEEN THERE DONE THAT

1. *Bringing Up Baby*

2. *A Lion in Winter*

3. Spencer Tracy

4. Labeled "Box Office Poison"

1. *The Princess and the Pirate* and *The Seven Little Foys*

2. Home in Palm Springs

3. "Thanks for the Memories"

4. Enjoyed boxing before show business

67

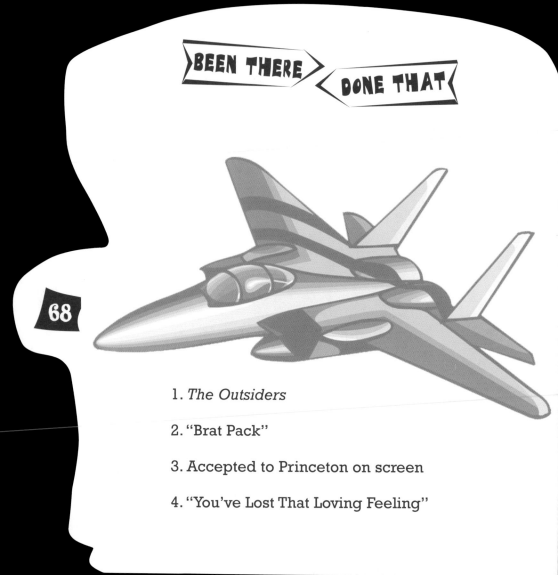

BEEN THERE DONE THAT

68

1. *The Outsiders*

2. "Brat Pack"

3. Accepted to Princeton on screen

4. "You've Lost That Loving Feeling"

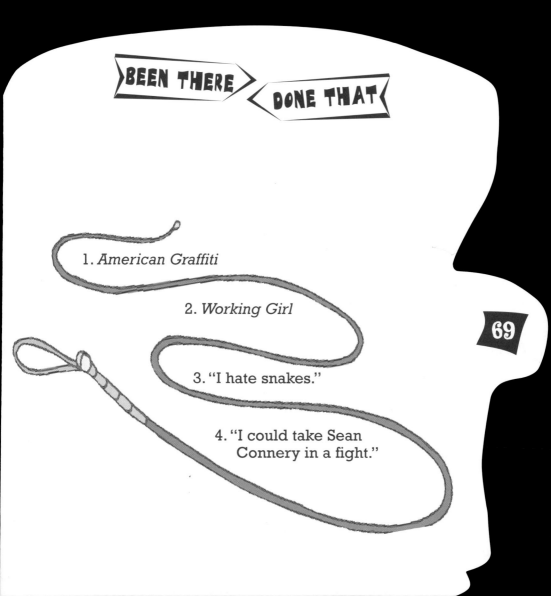

1. *American Graffiti*

2. *Working Girl*

3. "I hate snakes."

4. "I could take Sean Connery in a fight."

70

1. *Sabrina*

2. *To Have and Have Not*

3. "Of all the gin joints…"

4. Rick's Café Américain

1. *Desperately Seeking Susan*

2. *Who's That Girl?*

3. Breathless Mahoney

4. "Papa don't preach, I'm in trouble deep."

BEEN THERE > < DONE THAT

72

1. *Suspect*

2. "Gypsies, Tramps & Thieves"

3. *Moonstruck*

4. Chastity

1. *Cat on a Hot Tin Roof*

2. *The Sting*

3. "Don't ever hit your mother with a shovel. It leaves a bad impression on her mind."

73

4. Popcorn, spaghetti sauce and salad dressing

1. Pink Cadillacs

2. Ed Sullivan

3. *Viva Las Vegas*

4. "Suspicious
   Minds"

74

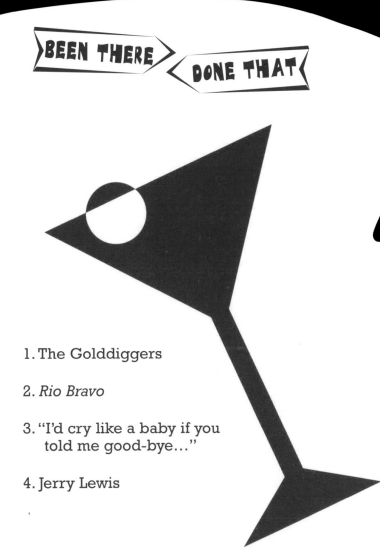

BEEN THERE DONE THAT

75

1. The Golddiggers

2. *Rio Bravo*

3. "I'd cry like a baby if you told me good-bye…"

4. Jerry Lewis

1. *The Wiz*

2. "Love Child"

3. Florence Ballard

4. "Through the mirror of
   my mind, time after time…"

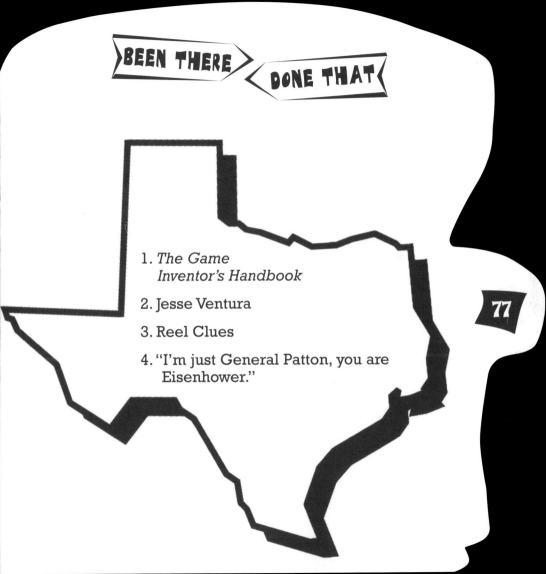

1. *The Game Inventor's Handbook*

2. Jesse Ventura

3. Reel Clues

4. "I'm just General Patton, you are Eisenhower."

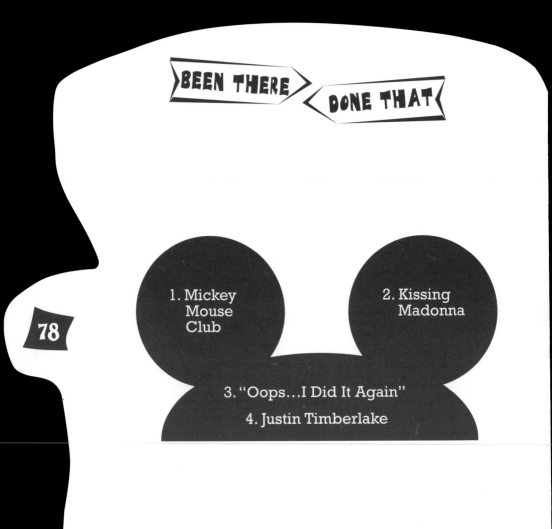

BEEN THERE DONE THAT

78

1. Mickey Mouse Club

2. Kissing Madonna

3. "Oops...I Did It Again"

4. Justin Timberlake

1. The Joey Bishop Show
2. Notre Dame's Fighting Irish
3. Kathy Lee, Kelly and Gelman
4. "Is that your final answer?"

1. Indianapolis, Indiana

2. *The Afternoon Show*

3. Velcro Man

4. "Will it float?"

BEEN THERE > < DONE THAT

1. *Rebel Without a Cause*

2. Appeared in old TV Westerns

3. *Hoosiers*

4. "We did it, man. We did it, we did it. We're rich, man. We're retirin' in Florida now, mister."

81

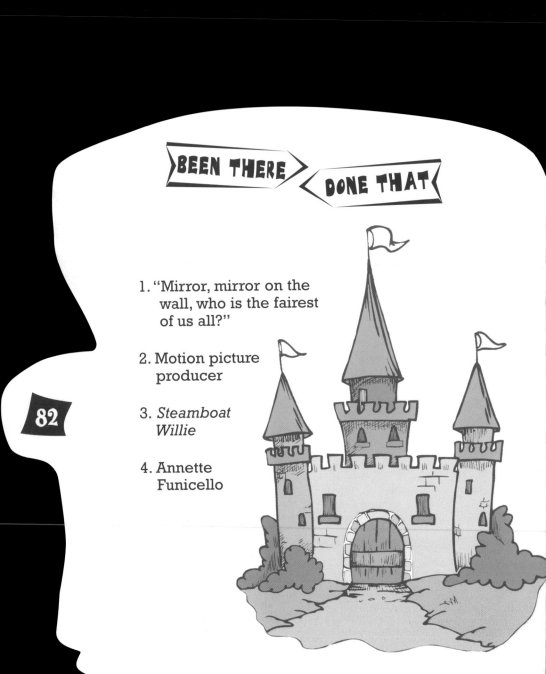

1. "Mirror, mirror on the wall, who is the fairest of us all?"

2. Motion picture producer

3. *Steamboat Willie*

4. Annette Funicello

BEEN THERE DONE THAT

1. Famous film director

2. *Psycho* and *Family Plot*

3. "Good evening."

4. "Funeral March of a Marionette"

BEEN THERE > < DONE THAT

84

1. Loyal soldier in Boer War

2. Yalta Conference with Roosevelt and Stalin

3. "The Iron Curtain"

4. Cigar smoker

BEEN THERE DONE THAT

1. *Spin City*

2. Bud Fox

3. Emilio Estevez

4. "I think now, looking back, we did not fight the enemy – we fought ourselves. The enemy was in us."

BEEN THERE > < DONE THAT

1. "Like Steve McQueen, all I need's a fast machine…"

2. *Tuesday Night Music Club*

3. "All I Wanna Do"

4. Kennett, Missouri

BEEN THERE DONE THAT

1. "Got a wife and kids in Baltimore, Jack…"

2. Asbury Park

3. "The Boss"

4. Nebraska

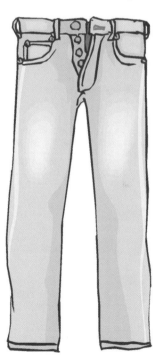

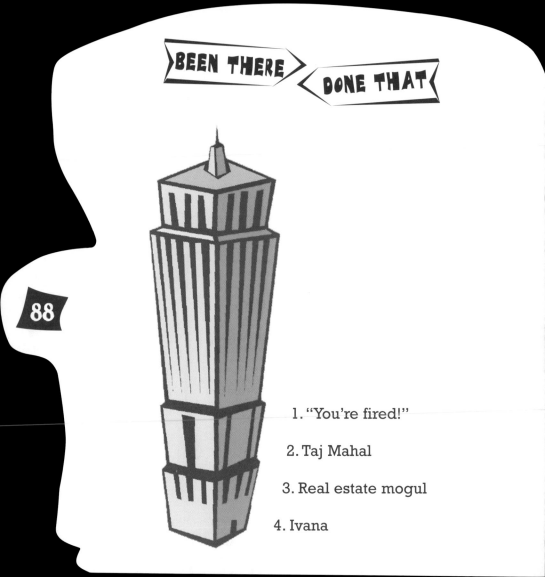

1. "You're fired!"

2. Taj Mahal

3. Real estate mogul

4. Ivana

1. "Heeeere's Johnny!"

2. *Easy Rider*

3. Angelica Huston

4. Randle Patrick McMurphy

90

1. Margaritas

2. *A Pirate Looks at Fifty*

3. "The weather is here, I wish you were beautiful."

4. The Coral Reefers

1. "Danger Prone" Daphne Blake

2. *All My Children*

3. Freddie Prinze Jr.

4. *I Know What You Did Last Summer*

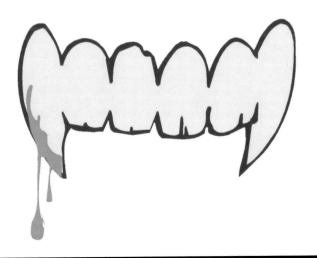

BEEN THERE DONE THAT

TAXI

92

1. TriBeCa Films

2. "You talkin' to me? You talkin' to me?"

3. Jake LaMotta

4. The Mafia

Solutions

Get a Clue

8   Mel Gibson

9   John Grisham

10 Cal Ripken

11 Jim Henson

12 Julia Roberts

13 Martin Scorsese

14 Andy Warhol

15 Stevie Wonder

16 Martin Luther King Jr.

17 Venus Williams

18 John Lennon

19 Tom Hanks

20 Michael Jordan

21 Meg Ryan

22 Woody Allen

23 Judy Garland

24 Marilyn Monroe

25 Shirley Temple Black

26 Angelina Jolie

27 Franklin Delano Roosevelt

28 Dr. Seuss (Theodore Geisel)

29 Tom Petty

30 Aretha Franklin

31 Ashton Kutcher

32 Martha Stewart

33 Sean Astin

34 Nicole Kidman

35 Ben Stiller

36 Brad Pitt

Solutions

Mysterious Musings

Solutions
Been There, Done That

95

ABOUT THE AUTHOR

Bob Moog, co-founder of University Games and publisher of Spinner Books, has been creating games, brainteasers, word puzzles and the like since childhood. He tormented his four younger siblings with quizzes, conundrums and physical and mental challenges during the 1960s. Now Moog brings his wacky, warped sense of humor and arcane knowledge about people into your hands with *Secret Identities.*

Moog is the author of several other puzzle, game and children's books, including *Gummy Bear Goes to Camp, 20 Questions, 30 Second Mysteries* and *Truth or Dare.*